F.A.B
FAITHFUL *Anchored* BLESSED
USING MY ENTIRETY TO PUSH THROUGH STORMS, WITH GOD

By

KERRY-ANN FACEY

F.A.B
FAITHFUL ANCHORED BLESSED

Scripture quotations are taken from the Holy Bible.

Scripture quotations marked NKJV are taken from the New King James Version®. Copyright © 1982 by Thomas Nelson.

Used by permission. All rights reserved

Scripture quotations marked NIV are taken from the New International Version®. Copyright© 1973, 1978, 1984, 2011 by Biblica, Inc.®

Used by permission. All rights reserved

Scripture quotations marked NLT are taken from the New Living Translation. Copyright© 1996, 2004, 2015 by Tyndale House Foundation. Used by permission of Tyndale House Publishers Inc., Carol Stream, Illinois 60188. All rights reserved.

Copyright © 2022 by Kerry-Ann Facey

All rights reserved. No part of this book may be reproduced or used in any manner without the written permission of the copyright owner except for the use of quotations in a book review. For more information, contact:

faithfulanchoredblessed@gmail.com

First paperback edition February 2022

Book illustration and design by Kamar Martin
Back Cover author photo by Atalia's Photos

ISBN 978-1-9990240-2-4 (Paperback)
ISBN 978-1-9990240-3-1 (eBook)

DEDICATION

This book is dedicated to my three beautiful children.

Kasia, Kalista and Kyzic

I thank our Father in Heaven, for choosing me to be your mother, giving me the ongoing strength and patience to raise you all and blessing me with the three most incredible blessings a woman could ever dream, vision and pray for.

You three are the reasons why the trajectory of my life and what I strive to give you bring me so much joy.

Look what Mommy did.

Look what the Lord has done.

With God, all things are possible!

"Shout To The Lord" - Hillsong Worship

CONTENTS

CHAPTER One: She Understood the Assignment -God 1

CHAPTER Two: Praise Report 2

CHAPTER Three: Fearfully and Wonderfully Made 3

CHAPTER Four: Have Your Way 6

CHAPTER Five: Wonderous Works in the Wait 8

CHAPTER Six: Refreshed Mental Mess 17

CHAPTER Seven: Taken Off the "Weight List" 22

CHAPTER Eight: Wayward Worrier to Fervent
                     Prayer Warrior 25

CHAPTER Nine: Secured Destination Point 29

CHAPTER Ten: Broken Focus Shifted to A Visual Paradise.... 33

CHAPTER Eleven: The Tune Up 37

CHAPTER Twelve: Conference Call... 45

CHAPTER Thirteen: Purpose Recalculated 49

CHAPTER Fourteen: The Best, Nothing Less 52

CONTENTS

CHAPTER Fifteen: Abundant Life, Access Granted,
.... More In Store 56

CHAPTER Sixteen: No Distance In Prayer 57

PEACE - BROKEN CHAINS - FREEDOM - VICTORY 59

ABOUT THE AUTHOR 60

CHAPTER ONE

She Understood the Assignment -God

"Lord, I'm Available To You" - The Gospel Project

Writing this book was a kingdom assignment and not just an opportunity. I was given and accepted divine instruction, and it is my duty to always obey. So, I stepped boldly into God's calling, where fear has no effect over my life.

So this is me walking in my confidence, sharing my story and blessing others, all while giving God the glory. I thank God for choosing and grooming me to complete this mission.

To do good and to use my journey as a testimony, to encourage others to trust God with their entirety. Not everyone is meant to support or understand your assignment, but be not discouraged. Heaven's endorsement is and always will be far greater than man's approval will ever be. I have confidence in the strength that God has instilled within me, that this book will touch someone's heart the way God intended it to.

"She speaks with wisdom and faithful instruction is on her tongue." - Proverbs 31: 2 NIV

CHAPTER TWO

Praise Report

"Yes Lord, Yes" - Shirley Caesar

I thank you for choosing this book. It is a testimony of my life, walking in my faith and confidence, all with God's strength.

I invite the Holy Spirit within your presence. I pray that anyone after reading this book will walk in their truth every moment of their lives. Our most High is worthy of our trust. I pray that the Lord will grant you a clear mind, open your heart and mind and that you will receive something anew from even at the minimum, one line within it.

I pray this book will be a blessing to you as it was an unimaginable blessing for me to have written it. In Jesus' name I pray, amen.

"Commit your actions to the Lord and your plans will succeed." - Proverbs 16:3 NLT

CHAPTER THREE

Fearfully and Wonderfully Made

"I Am Loved" - Maverick City Music

Glory be to God for everything that I am and everything I never imagined I would be.

My growth game is strong. One day I just woke up—different. Allow me to (re) introduce myself.

I am a proud mother and honored to be chosen as the mother of three beautiful children.

I am a proud owner of a licensed preschool enrichment program.

I am a daughter.

I am a sister; a baby sister at that. Yes, I am a big deal.

I am a proud auntie.

I am a friend.

I am a domestic violence survivor.

I am a warrior.

I am a force to be reckoned with.

Most importantly—

I am worthy.

I am enough.

I am a walking testimony.

I am rooted and grounded in love.

I am unashamed.

I am the head and not the tail.

I am above and not beneath.

I am a child of God.

I am God's masterpiece.

I am the daughter of a king.

I am worthy of being loved, and I am so loved.

Now, I am a publisher and an author.

To some, this may seem ordinary. And to others, they know THIS was a journey.

God has given me the authority to know and declare unequivocally who I am, and who I am to him, made in his image. And so I'm all those things and even so much more. I am not saying that I am better than anyone else. I am simply saying I am no less than anyone else. Let me let you in on something that you may or may not know. You, too, are all these things and so much more. You need to remind yourself of these things every day. Why? Because the truth stands behind its words.

To the best of my ability, I make a conscious effort each day to portray the Nine Fruits of the Spirit *(Galatians 5: 22-23)*. I express love, joy, peace, patience, kindness, goodness, faithfulness, gentleness and self-control. Sometimes, possessing these attributes allows you to be misunderstood. You can either end up being taken advantage of, or (hand up) become a product of manipulation. Sometimes, others may disagree that you dare to declare how you stand in confidence with the fruits, but it's natural for there to be misconceptions and for those around or even not around you to give a side-eye.

Let them. Here's a tip—you don't have to like who you see nor believe that someone is who they say they are, but try, at least try, to keep your misconceptions to yourself. It can break down someone who is and strives to be true (hand up—again). There are, believe it or not, a good chunk of people who do make a conscious effort to walk right. I am so grateful that I have reached a point in my life where I can take accountability, use discernment, and with confidence, conclude that not everyone is meant to be a part of my journey.

It wasn't until I began to write this book, did I come to the revelation that I am F.A.B. — faithful, anchored and blessed. I wanted to reach out to the multitudes to share the gospel and encourage that you too are just the same.

> *" Let your light so shine before men, that they may see your good works, and glorify your Father which is in heaven." - Matthew 5: 15-16 KJV*

CHAPTER FOUR

Have Your Way

"Tis So Sweet To Trust In Jesus" - Casting Crowns

Remember in the book of **Luke 5:4** when Jesus told Simon to push his boat into the water and told him to go deeper and let down his nets to catch fish? Well, that is also my story. God wanted to push me to do more, and I was comfortable in doubt. I hesitated many times. Truthfully, I have been disobedient. However, I kept getting signs and confirmations in various forms. But God always knows the situation and the outcome, so I had to trust him with all my heart. Here I am writing a book. Truthfully, I experienced many spiritual attacks for doing this, but regardless, God is faithful. So, I let down my net and let God be in control and look— I'm about to reach more than I will have the ability to carry! Amen.

As a Christian, sometimes we do things that don't make sense, or we feel like we shouldn't be doing things that don't make sense.

BUT GOD

God told me to let down my net for something that didn't make any sense to me. I truly haven't let my net down much in life.

My preschool, I let down my net and God has blessed me!

My ex-husband. After seventeen years, I let down that net too. I finally left. Another area in my life, after I made that move, God moved. Oh, the clarity. And it's also the main reason why and how I have this book to share my story and encourage others.

I am learning to trust the process and allow the Holy Spirit to lead me, even when the assignment doesn't appear possible, because he is so faithful. Taking a leap of faith can lead us to many blessings we wouldn't believe God can do.

> *"Trust in the Lord with all your heart,*
> *And lean not on your own understanding; In all your*
> *ways acknowledge Him,*
> *And He shall direct your paths."*
> *- PROVERBS 3:5-6 NKJV*

CHAPTER FIVE

Wonderous Works in the Wait

"At the right time, I, the Lord, will make it happen."
- Isaiah 60:22 NLT

"Wait On You" Elevation Worship & Maverick City Music

I pray about everything. And I don't make any moves without praying about a situation, decision or interaction first. Then I pray to our three in one God: Father, Son and Holy Spirit, present EVERYTHING and then, I wait.

Throughout my past dysfunctional relationship, I would often say that I would have to write a book because of the many events that occurred throughout. Of course, I said this without any seriousness at all until my "haha" moments became the truth.

Many times, I thought it was time to write this book, and it wasn't. Every time I tried, I drew a blank. No thoughts, no words, the pen wouldn't even move. I heard God say it wasn't time. He said, "Not now." So, I prayed and fasted and asked God to assure me when the time would be right. I admit, there are moments where I struggle with God's timing and his marvelous plans for me. I sometimes like to be in control, and when I cannot see where God is taking me or where it will lead me, apprehension begins to set in fast.

I knew that patience was key for this journey and that I needed to be obedient to God's time and not mine. However long that would take was out of my control. Time went on, and I began to think, maybe this isn't an assignment for me to accomplish. But I continued to pray and wait and begged God for an answer.

One night as I was praying, I received God's confirmation! It was loud and clear. "My daughter, you have waited on me. I have seen your patience and you have obeyed my words. You are an upcoming book author. Wait and see. I am with you. It is time."

Say what? I waited two years for this green light! I will remember that night like it was yesterday.

I was and still am so thankful to God for his approval and speaking into my eardrum as if he had a megaphone placed right into it.

God is never offended by us asking for confirmations repeatedly. It takes a lot of prayer. It takes a lot of sitting in his presence to confirm what we discussed privately with one another. And while we wait, you will be reminded that waiting is not in vain. It will not be a waste. God is working everything out for us in the waiting season. Sometimes we may feel that waiting is a punishment, when it is far from. It is a process. Our redeemer is always doing more than what we can see. Trust the process.

I give God all the glory for all the things he has done in my life. And for all the things that he will continue to do with increased favour, provision, and blessings—exceedingly and abundantly more than I can imagine. God has carried me through so many storms, struggles, close calls in my life that the only valid explanation of why I'm here and why I can humbly share my story with all of you is simply because of Him. I came to the revelation that God wanted me to wait to bring this book to life, not because he wanted to keep it from me but more so because he wanted to work something in me.

His grace and his mercy are what have brought me through.

Writing this book is one of the most vulnerable things I believe I have ever done. But it is also one of the most rewarding and fulfilling. Listen, I've been through a lot. More than anyone has imagined, can comprehend, or assumed I was, simply because I was hiding behind strained smiles and "The 'Gram." Yes, I was a wife. Yes, I am a mother. Yes, I was a mess. I was torn apart. I was abused physically, emotionally, spiritually, mentally, financially, and sexually for the entire relationship. I was alone, even while having someone sitting right next to me. I was depressed, anxious and confused. I was so hurt.

The relationship was so complicated that there were many times I wondered if it was even worth being here. Admittedly, it was that bad. But everything changed when I decided to take a step back and look at the larger picture. I decided to recommit myself to God. When I decided to give the apology to my heavenly Father that He didn't even need, I did it over and over again. I felt like I disappointed him for so many years. One thing I can say is that I truly don't regret any part of my life. If I did, you wouldn't have this book, and I wouldn't be sharing a snippet of my story. Neither would I be able to share how to be patient, trust and obey God from head to toe, all while feeling like you're falling apart. It takes time. Everything takes time. And I don't know about you, but I wouldn't be able to do what I have done or make it through that relationship without God being ever so loving and patient with me.

I'll give you a little bit of insight; the Coles' note version of how I went from burdens to blessings. I was in a very long relationship—sixteen years to be exact—with an extreme narcissist. Yes, the father of my three absolutely beautiful children. We were married for eight years and we cohabited for sixteen, but it was, for lack of a better word, hell.

Scripture reads: *"He who finds a wife finds a good thing."*
- **Proverbs 18:22**

Evidently, my ex-spouse was not aware of this. It wasn't until I decided to take a stand and surrender myself to God that I realized it was time for me to make a dramatic change. My ex-husband and I couldn't agree on important things, including a spiritual journey, which was difficult for me in the relationship. It was hard to be with someone who was saying the opposite of what I was saying spiritually. I tried to encourage him, but it was a dead-end road. I didn't see any effort through my ex-husband to grow and please God. Eventually, I stopped.

> *"If anyone will not welcome you or listen to your words, leave that home or town and shake the dust off your feet." - Matthew 10:14*

We know that in order to have a strong and healthy relationship, God has to be in the centre to connect the two of you.

Scripture teaches us: *"How can two walk together unless they agree?"* **- Amos 3:3**

Furthermore, *"Do not be yoked together with unbelievers." -* **2 Corinthians 6:14 NIV**

The repercussions of staying in an unequally yoked relationship can cause more self-sabotage than we may be open to admitting.

I wish I knew then what I know now, but again, everything takes time. My ex-husband needed to see God for himself. I could encourage him as much as I wanted to, but if he didn't want to have a relationship with Him, my words were just being used in vain. He needed to be led by God to lead a family. He needed to be dedicated to God because then he would have known how to resist temptations. We did not agree on basically everything, and I was never interested in what he was, because: *"I will not look with approval on anything that is vile. I hate what faithless people do; I will have no part in it." - Psalms 101:3*

This was my stance within the relationship.

> *"A person without self-control is like a city with broken-down walls." - Proverbs 25:28 NLT*

Self-control is what he lacked. A broken relationship is what we gained.

A partner needs to respect God because a man/woman that respects God will respect you. They must know how to get into God's presence. I wish I had known that I should never allow a man driven by lust to enter my space. I wish I had known not to connect with a non-believer, or else they would lead me astray. I wish I had known that I should have run if someone was controlling, manipulative or abusive. I had a lukewarm spouse. I was not his mother, and I simply was trying to introduce him to the God I serve. Through that relationship, there were many things that happened that I may not be particularly proud of, but again, it's what has brought me to where I am right now and has enabled me to begin again. I was starting to compromise myself spiritually for him. I was not growing, and I stopped pursuing God. My life was in utter devastation because I was in a relationship with this person. I was worried more about pleasing my ex-husband, and I was least worried about pleasing God. I moved away from God, and I had to try and keep this ex happy. That was not God's will for me. He caused me to stumble spiritually for far too long, and that wasn't going to work either. It took me nearly seventeen years to realize that my ex-husband was the cause of me substituting him for God and it came to a point where I realized that wasn't going to lead to a life of purpose. I chose not to settle. I chose not to let someone get in my way of building my relationship with God simply to please them. I am far better off being bored or lonely for a temporary amount of time, than to stay in a relationship because of "time served." That will lead me straight to hell. Anyone sent my way is supposed to bring me closer to my purpose, and if it's pulling me towards sin, then they are disguised as the enemy and are a complete distraction.

My life was SPIRALING. I told myself, "Keep your eyes on Jesus, Kerry-Ann. Stay focused on Him, Kerry-Ann. He is going to bring you out of this! You are worth so much more."

Trust me when I say God <u>will</u> show you the way. He will heal you, strengthen you and give you all the things you need. It is not God's plan for anyone on this earth to be alone. So, if that's something you're worried about, don't be. Be more concerned with embracing your season of singleness, preparation, waiting, knowing, praying for your future forever and trusting God that He will send someone who chases Him and will know how to love you because he loves God first!

DO NOT SETTLE. Wait for that person who will push you towards your purpose rather than pull you away from your destiny. It's never easy to start over, but when I look back to where I was and where I am now, I give Him all the praise because God was and will always be in the midst. But our flesh will allow us to do things that aren't his will or plan for our lives and what he did not put his hands on from the start.

My children's father will always be in my prayers, and I will always call his name to God. I will always pray for his protection and healing, but I will never find myself in a situation like that ever, ever again! Amen! He and I together was not God's will. God allows free will. We can all agree that we tend to pursue relationships that may appear convenient versus fulfilling and purposeful rather than trusting God and all the unimaginable things he desires for us to begin with. That relationship has revealed to me who I am, taught me how to be a better person and be someone better for someone else. It taught me how to strive for a Christ-like union. The relationship also taught me how to be the best version of myself for my children. One thing I know, there's always favour after failure, and for that reason, I give God all the praise.

Don't ever confuse burdens and blessings, nor allow yourself to go spiritually bankrupt by investing in someone who God never intended you to be with.

There is a huge difference! I now know how to distinguish and look for purpose, purity and modesty in a man, and I now know that a man driven by God in the Holy Spirit is truly heaven sent and worth the wait.

It takes all of you to stand in obedience to God and be patient as we wait. I know it seems impossible, but it isn't as complex as it seems. I will share a few of my experiences as a testimony to serve as an encouragement to trust God with your entirety. Be patient for God's will and obey Him even though things may feel like they're completely falling apart. Even when it looks like things are spiralling out of control and you begin to wonder if life can get any worse. Life will throw us a million curveballs, and it may feel like one of the worst games of dodgeball you've ever played in, but trust God. Obey God. Have crazy faith that God will come through for you. His promises are true, and he is so faithful. But faith without work is dead, and this is your weighted wait training right here. Commit, surrender and put all your problems at God's feet and trust that He will come through for you just as he promised.

Even with faith as small as a mustard seed, all things are possible. I can recall the many instances when I truly believed I had all the answers. I would take things into my control and use my God-given authority in the wrong context to say, "You know what God? I got this! I know you said this, but I'm going to do this instead. There is no way this situation will turn out well if I don't just do this."

How many times did I say that? And how many times did my boisterous self blow up in my face? Too many times to count. Until it felt as though God hit me on the side of the head like a good old V8 commercial and knocked some sense into me. I had no other choice but to BE STILL.

> *"The Lord will fight for you. All you have to do is keep still."* **- Exodus 14:14 NLV**

What does this mean? Put yourself on a time-out. Run to God and do not rely on your strength alone. How do we know if we believe that God is good? Ask yourself, how well do you trust him when life isn't going the way you want it to go, expect it to go or need it to go.

Believe that God is good even when people leave your life, when you don't get the promotion or when life gets rough. Believe that God is good all the time and...

BE STILL.

"Be still, and know that I am God"

- Psalms 46:10 NKJV

CHAPTER SIX

Refreshed Mental Mess

"I've Got My Mind Made Up" - Donnie McClurkin

One of the hardest things to do is trust someone. The minute something goes wrong in our lives, the first part of our body that begins to hurt us most is our mind—the thoughts in our head. Our minds began to fill with so many different scenarios and it simply does not let us rest. What if this happens? What if that happens? What if I don't get that? What am I going to do? We start to process so many things, and we begin to get lost in our thoughts. Anxiety, internalized stress and fear begin to welcome themselves in.

I battled with anxiety and depression for four years (I was medically diagnosed). I was on medication as a part of treatment for my anxiety. Thankful to declare, I've been anxiety and depression free for the past four years—glory to God! But little did I remember that the one true cure was to become the kind of person who ALREADY trusts our Heavenly Father and to walk with Jesus in the Kingdom of God when stressors came.

I was so fixated on all of the troubles I had, which were all surrounded by my relationship.

Time for transparency. My ex-husband was a liar, cheater, manipulator, addicted to pornography and a narcissist at its best. Day in and day out, my anxiety was through the roof. I was restless, easily agitated and heavy burdened. My mind wasn't calm, neither was my body. Sleep? Ha. What was that? I could not sleep due to the fear of nightmares or flashbacks of things that had happened and had traumatized me. I had low self esteem. I was insecure. I felt as if I wasn't enough, so I was always trying to please The Mister.

The word tells us:

> *"Do not be anxious about anything, but in every situation, by prayer and petition, with thanksgiving, present your requests to God".* - **Philippians 4:6 NIV**

I get anxious just reading this scripture. The picture-perfect marriage wasn't so pretty. How was I not to be troubled? I closed the book.

I felt so defeated already, and I didn't even try to listen to God's words. I felt like I had already failed him as his daughter, and I would never be able to do as he said. Life was SO bad. How in the world was He going to fix it and fix me?

I didn't give the Bible a chance, and I harmed myself in the process. I was fighting myself by doing so. And by also denying my feelings and believing that this life was the be-all end-all.

You see, the enemy wants you to believe that you are the opposite of who God says you are. He wants you to think that you are unworthy. He wants you to believe you're a failure. Your nemesis wants you to think that you will never be forgiven. He wants you to think that there is no hope in your future—and it's all a lie. But the truth of the matter is, God wants us to experience his peace and trust Him in all things.

It came to the point that I realized my anxiety was taking complete control of my day-to-day routine, and I couldn't handle the weight. "I can't take this anymore. I can't do this on my own. I need you. I'm giving this all to you, my Lord. Heal my mind. YOU fix it." That was it. Handing over the crazy life to Him and praying that He would fill my head with peace was all I wanted.

Bit by bit, I learned to calm down my anxious mind.

I learned patience. That was not easy. Being a spectator of my husband as he continued his nonsense, while I stood in obedience, was HARD. But I needed to regain strength, and I wanted it right away—not tomorrow but today. I needed to accept the fact that I was a mess. That my life wasn't the way I thought it would be, but healing and peace would come through a process.

I did not have the mental capacity to navigate the thoughts in my head or to draw up solutions one by one for each of the trails I was enduring. I finally learned to talk about my emotions. I sought counselling, and I also brought my troubles to my saviour. I felt less anxious when I talked through my feelings. By doing this, I felt lighter. The weight from my mind wasn't an impending boom as it always was. My ex-husband never gave me the opportunity to have the right to my emotions. Instead, he was forever defensive and dismissive.

BUT GOD

He cares for us, and He hears the words we say in our thoughts when we cannot speak. Through prayer and petition, for the first time I felt that my feelings were real and valid. His words gave me the encouragement that I was longing for when I was finding the peace I never knew I would ever find.

We need to remember to verbalize our issues to Him. He is so F.A.B. Period.

Remember when Jesus was in the boat on the sea of Galilee, and a storm came rolling in? Everyone was frantic. Jesus just laid there wondering what was up with these men.

He rebuked the wind and said to the waves:

> ***"Peace, be still". - Mark 4:39 KJV***

Jesus was so calm because he used his authority and trusted his father to cease the weighted sea. God the Father, the Son and the Holy Spirit will calm your body from head to toe when you are face to face with weighted struggles. We need to try and strive to be more like Jesus. Entrusting our lives and well-being to the only one who can lift the weight.

Trust that the Lord is sovereign!

I'm building up my confidence more than I have ever done before. I reached a higher level and a new appreciation for myself, and I love myself more than I ever have. I can genuinely say that I feel more beautiful than I did in a sixteen-year relationship. I feel more desirable. I feel more confident. I look in the mirror and smile rather than pass a mirror while holding my head down.

God gives us a different strength mentally when we choose to stick and focus on his words. Pray to God consistently and ask him to help you trust him, heal and clear your mind so you may seek Him in all that you do. The only way to get through a weighted wait period of any struggle and declare what you want the outcome to be is to fill your mind with declarations of peace and joy.

Take hold of your helmet of salvation and invade your thoughts with his promises. Be amazed at what he will do. The enemy will always try to attack our intellectual capabilities. Our job is to protect our minds spiritually from the mighty blows of doubt and shame of the enemy.

> *"Therefore I say to you, whatever things you ask when you pray, believe that you receive them, and you will have them." - Mark 11:24 NKJV*

CHAPTER SEVEN

Taken Off the "Weight List"

"Lean On You" - Chandler Moore

Common expression: the weight of the world is on your shoulders. That was my marriage as a whole. The life of a wife, mother, daughter, sister, entrepreneur, friend made me feel as if everything was pressing down on me and at times it felt like I literally could not get up. My marriage carried me back to when I was in school, wearing a backpack filled to the zip with multiple projects and assignments. I carried so many responsibilities. I felt like I had a heavy barbell resting on me—which I couldn't, even if I tried— lift and the weight on my shoulders left me with a hunch back and poor posture. All things pertaining to the family were my responsibility. My thought process was that if my spouse wouldn't do it, then I had no choice. I could do all things through Christ that strengthens me, but I never asked myself why should I? There's a lot to carry. It's a lot to hold on to and it makes you wonder when will it ever end? When will we have a breakthrough?

BUT GOD

God doesn't want us to hold any burdens on our shoulders. He is here to carry the weight while we wait for our miracles, breakthroughs, visions and revelations that He promised us to happen. He wants you to trust him and know that it is well. I bent over backwards to make ends meet, not fully committing and trusting God because it didn't seem like the way I wanted it to be.

God invites us to lay down the burdens we carry and cast them upon his most capable shoulders. We tend to forget that Jesus carried a 165-pound cross on his shoulders for forty minutes to save us from our sins. He is built to withstand even the heaviest burdens. Always remember, as one of God's most beautiful creations, we need to be patient. Obey Him and trust that He will carry us through. We don't need to carry any heaviness with us. Trust Him and rely on his strength to carry our load so that you can stand tall and strong. Just as I do now, ask God to forgive us for trying to be macho and taking on more than we can bear. Pray, trust, and let God release the weight from your shoulders as you wait in obedience for your seasonal storm to cease. Be faithful to him as he is to you.

Saints, do not lose your posture. How easily we forget to cast our burdens unto the Lord, He cares for you. The progress to the promise may often shift your position, but whatever you do, stay grounded from head to toe. Continue to worship, praise and seek Him in all your ways. Your tears, your cries,—they are not in vain. Our Heavenly Father sees and hears you and cares deeply about you. Testimonies, more often than we recall, do come with a test.

You are far too close to the finish line of your victorious breakthrough. Let your thoughts of giving up now be removed in Jesus' name. Shoulders up, back and down. Stand tall and straight in your authority.

He is the world-renowned heavy-weight champion.

> *"Come to me, all of you who are weary and carry heavy burdens, and I will give you rest."*
> *- Matthew 11:28-30 NLT*

CHAPTER EIGHT

Wayward Worrier to Fervent Prayer Warrior

"Falling On My Knees" - **William McDowell**

It felt as if every moment with my ex-husband was bringing me to my knees throughout my lengthy relationship. It was getting harder and harder every day. And, more times than I would like to admit, I would ask God why he was punishing me. God wasn't punishing me at all. Sometimes we put ourselves in situations without seeking God first, and then the storms roll through one after another.

Let me clarify a subject before moving forward. Praying on our knees is not the only way or "right way" to pray. It doesn't make God answer our prayers any better or any quicker, nor does it make him answer our prayers at all. Neither does prayer require us to use eloquent speech. Our body posture has no effect on our prayers, but rather, it is the posture of our heart—the condition of our souls. Once your heart and soul are one with God, one can pray in any posture imaginable. The whole point is to communicate with him.

For myself, kneeling to God was the only posture I knew best.

At the beginning of this chapter, I expressed how I felt as if my relationship brought me down to my knees. I would go on my knees and beg and plead for Him to change my ex-partner, to perform a miracle, something. Those prayers soon turned into prayers of removing him from my life. I realized that HE had to want to change for himself and his family first. No matter what I did or said, his behaviour was out of my control. I no longer yearned for his attention. Instead, I yearned for him to have more time with God.

After many years, I realized that he was not the man God intended me to be with. Undoubtedly, we often hinder and delay God's plans for us, what he has in store for our lives and who he truly desires us to be with because we settle for what we believe is our only option. Never should we stay in a relationship because of time served. The self-inflicted trauma we pull ourselves into is far worse than we can imagine.

I was in such a dark place that I prayed endlessly, crying out to God daily on my knees. I was so broken. I could not think of any other strategy to get out of the mess. It was one battle, one storm, one trial after another. I had enough. I needed answers, grace, mercy, and I needed to be free. The impact was so heavy on my entire self that because I was so weak, to begin with, that I was already near my knees—so I just fell. I was so broken inside that my only choice was to get down on my knees and pray for God to comfort me.

Yes, God is sovereign and allows us to go through hardships to build our faith and trust and believe that He is who he says he is. God says that he is a gracious Heavenly Father who is faithful to hearing and answering his children's needs.

When I fall on my knees, it means war. However, I have seen many blessings come my way. Simply because when I fell to my knees, my God had mercy on me and lifted me.

David surrendered himself to God when Saul was hunting to kill him. God was the ultimate help that David needed. While David was hiding in the cave, David said:

> *"Have mercy on me, O God, have mercy! I look to you for protection.*
> *I will hide beneath the shadow of your wings until the danger passes by.*
> *I cry out to God Most High, to God who will fulfill his purpose for me." - Psalms 57:1-2 NLT*

I tried to get our relationship under control, but this wasn't a job for me to handle. My strength alone would never save me from the storms and hurricanes that blew in, including the ones that we create for ourselves.

BUT GOD

Fervent prayer will always bring you closer to the right areas in your life, the right community and the right opportunities. Even though you may not see or feel things working in your favour, believe that God works on your prayers and makes things happen for you.

He saved me, and He will surely do the same for you. Sometimes when life brings us to our knees, we should stay there in obedience to God.

We need to trust and know that His grace is sufficient, and He will carry us through.

> *"Don't worry about anything; instead, pray about everything.*
>
> *Tell God what you need and thank him for all he has done."* **- Philippians 4:6 NLT**

CHAPTER NINE

Secured Destination Point

"Just A Closer Walk With Thee" - The Worship Team

There were more times than I can count where I, quite literally, could not stand on my two feet throughout my past relationship. The feet that were meant to help me balance, walk, run, rise and lower my body instead were weak, unsure, treading lightly and always walking on eggshells. You see, I endured a lot more than I ever imagined I would have with my ex-husband. The abuse, disrespect, infidelity, gaslighting and extreme narcissistic behaviour were just a few of the reasons why I felt so insecure about where I was and where I was going. I didn't want to make any sudden moves out of fear of not knowing what I may be walking into. Not only did I fear where my steps would take me, but I was also restricted to where I could go. I was told where, when and with whom I could go. My walk-in life was not my own. My every move was dictated by someone who ate, slept and breathed control, and foolishly enough, I adhered to the "rules." Keeping the peace between him and me felt like the best option for everyone. Especially in the heat of everything my children and I were going through and what they were being exposed to. On the flip side, in his manipulative, unkind, and for lack of a better word—twisted mind frame, he felt victorious every time I complied with his requests. That lasted for seventeen years.

BUT GOD

Our feet are not only the foundation of our physical walk but our spiritual walk as well. A scripture in which I stand firmly on each day is from the book of Proverbs.

> *"Trust in the LORD with all your heart And lean not on your own understanding;*
> *In all your ways acknowledge Him, And He shall direct your paths." - Proverbs 3:5-6 NKJV*

My understanding did not see the overall big picture. My emotions would fluctuate, and my heart at times deceived me. I needed clear and concise guidance on what path to take. Not from a spouse who did not lead as he should, or did not acknowledge or understand **Proverbs 18:22** (*"He who finds a wife finds a good thing and receives favour from the Lord."*), but instead, the fulfilling guidance solely from my Heavenly Father. I spent so much time striving to submit to my husband, planning our lives and thinking of ways to impress him or keep his hands, eyes, and heart on me rather than dishonouring our marriage that I failed miserably.

Although people plan their course of life in their hearts, it is solely our Heavenly Father who establishes our steps. Ask God always to direct your steps. As much as we may think we can jumpstart God's plans for us, and He may have all the answers, we simply cannot do anything without Him giving us the strength to do it.

When I surrendered my all and all to Christ, I knew that I needed to anchor myself to Him and ask for mercy on me. For divine protection and grace for all the places that He will call me to go.

If you truly want to walk in faith with God, you will first need to, as I did, submit your fears to Him and accept the path he leads you through. You will learn how to be courageous, even when you are afraid and unsure of what lies ahead. Dig deep and ask God to guide your feet in the path of peace and blessing and to anoint you with the wisdom and knowledge of how to proceed, even when it seems as if you are walking on uneven grounds, dark streams of fear or muddy slopes. Ask Him to help you stand strong in his perfect will and in His words and lead you to see the sunrise no matter how it appears in your eyes. Not every delay is a downfall. Many times, God is often leading us to a better outcome. Learn to rejoice when things don't go as planned.

I have been out in the deep. And even though there are some bumps along the way, I still step strongly. The pep in my step is real. I used to tread lightly. Walk so softly. Tiptoe in and around people and things, not wanting to ever step on anyone's toes. But I cannot compare the liberating feeling I felt when I put my foot down to any other feeling I know.

The path behind me is dusty, uneven ground and is like empty woods. It stands alone. It is distant. The path ahead still has its bumps, but I kick those pebbles to the side and get to steppin'.

I am walking in God's will. With courage and fire under my feet and it feels so, so good.

If you ask God to guide your footsteps, be obedient to his instructions and be prepared to move your feet when he says to. Only then do we find ourselves winning the race and having the victory at the finish line.

> *"Mark out a straight path for your feet; stay on the safe path. Don't get sidetracked; keep your feet from following evil."*
> *- Proverbs 4: 26-27 NLT*

CHAPTER TEN

Broken Focus Shifted to A Visual Paradise

"God I Look To You" - Tasha Cobbs Leonard

I have witnessed a lot more than I had imagined I would have in my life as a whole. Many of which, at times, I still cannot remove the images from the forefront of my memory. I spent almost two decades with an individual who completely transformed day to day right before my eyes. Never in my wildest dreams would I have thought that someone could go from bad to worse so quickly. It felt like I was standing in front of a mirror watching a real-life movie—and the main characters were my family. I went to sleep at night praying I would wake up, and all of it was a dream, but every day, it seemed I continued to wake up within the same horror film.

I witnessed my ex-husband engage in various things which were sore to the eyes. I watched part of his family witness the same and turn a blind eye to the outrageous behaviours. It was the hardest thing to observe him destroying his family and everyone around him but even more so, damaging himself in the process. It wasn't easy to watch someone who was, and despite all we have been through is still important to me, to not make any positive changes right before my eyes. But I didn't want anything to do with him for a long time coming, and the time was finally here.

> **"But I say to you, love your enemies, bless them those who curse you, do good to those who hate you and pray for those who spitefully use you and persecute you."**
> **- Matthew 5:44 NKJV**

It wasn't long before I concluded that I didn't want to stand in front of this narcissistic monster (as I called him) anymore. Patterns of destructive behaviours—no, thank you.

I didn't want to see another hand raised, another back turned on myself and our children, being replaced with a new supply (aka somebody else) simply out of boredom or when I was being disrespectful. I no longer wanted to see financial recklessness. I didn't want any of it anymore. He never noticed the tears shed or the heartache I experienced and never realized nor admitted to his wrongs. I had enough. I needed to see things the way God saw it before my life continued to spiral out of control.

We need to ask the Lord to change our vision so we can see things through his lens, and in the same breath, ask for forgiveness for taking our eyes off Him.

Alter your vision, transform your heart and alter your position as a spectator. Transition into being viewed as a walking testimony, giving God the glory.

We need to remind ourselves that we are made in his image and nothing less.

For a long while, I thought the life I had was all the life I had to settle into.

Terrifying. I would not have wanted that life for anyone, and that is why I am here to encourage you, my friend. Or perhaps you will encourage a friend of a friend of a friend that when you need a changed perspective, bring it all to God. He WILL change your vision. He WILL give you a glimpse of what his plans for your life look like in his eyes. He wants to turn your pain into peace, and like myself, turn my mess into a message to share with others.

Now, I see things differently. No longer through the foggy, obscured lens that I was used to looking through. The Lord, our God is SO kind. He offers us all the privilege to see things in a new light.

A perfect passage from the Bible that can help to remember Jesus and his power, can be found in the book of *Luke when* Jesus healed a blind man:

> *"Receive your sight, your faith has healed you."*
> *- Luke 18:42 NIV*

The man at the side of the street was poor. He couldn't see. He couldn't work. But he had faith that Jesus would be the only one who could save him, so he called out to him for help.

In your seasons, when you feel like you are seeing darkness, have faith. Call out to Him. He may or may not answer in that instant, but I encourage you to continue to call out for his help without ceasing. Jesus used this miracle of the beggar to show us his power and what He can do. Through faith in Him, our eyes can be opened to things that we couldn't gain a full understanding of through natural means. Jesus enables us to see things differently, and through him doing just that, the way you choose to live your life can't help but be impacted.

I thank God each day for granting me his vision to eliminate all confusion in my life.

I praise Him for clarifying and adjusting my vision to see and know that the plans He has for me are far greater than what I was ready to settle with.

My future is bright. I can see it because I can see things the way God does. I cry tears of joy for what is to come. So don't forget to lift your eyes to him and do the same.

> *"So we don't look at the troubles we can see now; rather we fix our gaze on things that cannot be seen. For the things we see now will soon be gone, but the things we cannot see will last forever." - 2 Corinthians 4:18 NLT*

CHAPTER ELEVEN

The Tune Up

"Voice of God" - Dante Bowe featuring Steffany Gretzinger & Chandler Moore

Our ears play an essential part in our day-to-day life. A part of our bodies which provides us with the ability to hear. Good news, bad news, truth or lies, loudness or silence.

Sometimes we tend to forget just how blessed we are to have all our body parts and their functionality. Many use aids to hear, and for some, they are deaf.

Here comes openness. I suffered from slightly distorted hearing in one of my ears.

If you are reading this book and know me well enough, you may be having an "ah-ha" or rather an "Oh, shucks" moment. You may also be experiencing some guilt for the many times during a conversation when I said, pardon one, two or three times, and your response was, "Are you deaf?!" or "Never mind! I will tell you later!" or anything of that nature. Surprise. I simply could not hear you as clearly as you likely would assume I would have.

THE TUNE UP

It was in the year 2013. To this very day, should I need to revisit the event in my mind for reasons such as this, the replay is so vivid and saddening. Following the swift blow to my ear, the pain, the specs of red that came out, followed by gradual silence—left me numb.

What was this? Why did that happen? What's next? What have I done to deserve this? These were all questions I asked MYSELF. Not once did I ask God. I always loved my Heavenly Father and always will. However, at some point, I was ashamed I was still hanging on to a relationship that was damaging to the family, and quite literally, damaging to myself.

The signs were there, and I wasn't listening.

Close to the end of 2018, I began to hear a short and very soft whisper.

"It's time to let go."

It was during this time that a few months before, I was diagnosed with depression and anxiety. So, I concluded that perhaps it was the medication causing me to hear things.

Everywhere I would go, this whisper would be right there with me.

"It's time to let go. It's time to let go."

In the shower, I could hear this voice. Pull the curtains, no one was there.

Driving solo in the car. Backseat. There that voice was again. Pull over. No one there.

Then the whisper got louder and louder and louder and was now loud and clear. It was a shout and demand. The voice said, "LET GO!"

After a few months of this ever so clear statement, it dawned on me that the voice I heard had to be the voice of God.

I remember literally saying, "Oh my God! It's you! I can hear you!"

But what was He referring to was the next question? So, I began to ask for clarity.

After much thought, I realized that He could only be referring to my marriage. God had given me warning signs, sometimes extreme ones, and told me to turn around, leave and never look back. But I was caught up in emotions, and it became difficult to see the signs. As a result, I was stuck in an extremely unhealthy and toxic relationship for many years.

I am sure I am not the only one that can say I love marriage, and I love to love. But then we have someone who may simply love the concept of you but not you entirely.

I made the mistake of putting another person in the place where only God belongs. A relationship I chose without consulting God, rather than Him choosing for me. A man that led me to sin. A relationship where my connection with God should have been paramount in my heart. A relationship in which my choices should have been based on what pleases Him and how it affects my relationship with Him. It was a relationship where I was abused mentally, physically, emotionally, sexually, financially, and spiritually.

BUT GOD

God kept his hands on me time and time again. Sign after sign after sign.

Thank you, Lord! Let us give a shout of praise!

I spent far too long choosing to honour someone over choosing to honour God. And in turn, he didn't honour me. When I think about it and remind myself of what I have been through, it makes my stomach turn.

The Bible teaches us in 2 Corinthians 6:14 – NIV

> *"Be not unequally yoked together with unbelievers: for what fellowship hath righteousness with unrighteousness? And what communion hath light with darkness?"*

I was a believer, my ex-spouse—not so much. I thought that I could help draw him closer to God. Pray with him, for him, encourage him, but my efforts were in vain.

He told me I was in a cult. He said that I worshipped some white man. I had nothing left in me to try and convince him otherwise. What does the word say about this?

> *"Whoever does not welcome you, nor listen to your message, as you leave that house or city, shake the dust off your feet." - Matthew 10:14 NKJV*

I did my best to share God's promises and words with him, but it was time for me to dust off my feet and move on. The best thing I could do for myself and our children was to stop fighting for someone who evidently, was not afraid and was completely okay with losing me.

I spent some time speaking to anointed friends and members of the church and asked this one question: "How do I know if God is speaking to me or if it is the enemy?"

The common and only answer I received was that you would experience a lot of confusion, if it was the enemy. If it is God, once you follow through, there you will find peace.

I had a choice to make. I wavered between 'is it God or is it not,' for months. Finally, an extremely traumatic event occurred that I never in a million years would have imagined could have taken place. Following this event, I knew this was it. I didn't make a move for another two months, but just like an umpire, I needed to decide and stick to it. I finally did it. This was God. I was searching for hesitation, confusion—couldn't find it. The relief I felt at that moment, minutes, hours, days and months continued to follow me. We should keep in the back of our minds that everything in the Kingdom of God operates solely and surely under the directive of peace. The Lord spoke to me and instructed that I was to head in the direction that would give me the most peace. I dared to step out of indecision and into faith. The Lord gave me such confirmation and joy that I have never doubted the wisdom of that decision ever since. That one decision, possibly more than any other, set my life and my children's lives on a course that has brought us to where we are today. Amen!

Depression, anxiety, medication—gone. Husband. *swings baseball bat and knocks the ball out of sight*—gone.

My ears were open, and I could hear God's voice and obey his words, finally.

I believe that God does speak to us more than we acknowledge. However, it is the simple fact that we miss out on what He is saying because we are honestly not listening.

As I share this with you, it is everything that I, too, need to discipline myself to work on. We are not perfect, but instead progressing. I came to the revelation that all true believers can and do hear the voice of God; we just don't recognize it.

> When we listen for God, we might consider the following verse that is found in **1 Kings 19:11-13:**
>
> *"Then a great and powerful wind tore the mountains apart and shattered the rocks before the Lord, but the Lord was not in the wind. After the wind there was an earthquake, but the Lord was not in the earthquake. After the earthquake came a fire, but the Lord was not in the fire. And after the fire came a gentle whisper. When Elijah heard it, he pulled his cloak over his face and went out and stood at the mouth of the cave."*
>
> Did you notice that God's voice came to Elijah as a gentle whisper? We must be quiet to hear a whisper.

Or, when God called Samuel three times before he realized with the help of Eli that God was calling him.

I think, too, of how Jesus went away to "lonely places and prayed." *(Luke 5:16)*

And in ***Psalms 46:10 NKJV,*** **"Be still and know that I am God."**

In the stillness, not busyness, we tune our spiritual ears to hear his voice.

Stop and listen. Quiet your mind and listen for God to speak. Life often gets in the way, and amid all the turmoil of our daily lives, we cannot hear that still, small voice. We forget to make time to pause and get into God's presence, make space to focus on him and listen to the most important voice of all—the voice of God. It may reveal itself to you in various sources, but it will always find a way to you and will be repeated to you as well just as it was for me. We are all pros at speaking to Him, but as Christians, we often have a hard time hearing God's voice, and this is not the way the Lord intended it to be. Make it your duty to find a quiet space perfect for you and Him. God began whispering to me when my surroundings were quiet, until his whisper became a shout. And until I tuned in, it's was if He said, "Can you hear me now?" I also imagined an eye roll accompanying his question.

One of the most incredible things we have been blessed with has to be that of hearing God speak to us personally. Instead of going through life blindly, we can easily have the wisdom of God to guide, guard and protect us.

Our gracious Heavenly Father loves, helps us from bad relationships and speaks to every one of his children constantly, providing us with all the tools we need to be overcomers. But it is our responsibility to hear Him, trust Him and obey Him. We need to acknowledge the fact that we don't know everything.

The next time you are wondering whether the voice you hear is the voice of God, put it to the test. God won't contradict himself. We can measure everything based on scripture with what you believe he is saying to you. That will be the confirmation that you have, in fact, heard right.

Our listening ears to him are like a radio. There is never a problem with God's transmitter. It is the receiver that often needs help. My sister, my brother, tune in.

> ***"He who has ears to hear, let him hear!"***
> *- Matthew 11:15 NKJV*

CHAPTER TWELVE

Conference Call

"I Must Tell Jesus" - Sanchez

God tells us in his word that there is incredible power in the tongue. The words that come out of our mouths can be the most difficult part of our body to control. They can leave us with great regret if we use our words to hurt. Our tongues can bring both blessings and life curses.

I hold myself accountable and know the pain of regretting the words I have spoken.

My mouth in the past used to spit fire. Meaning, if I were angry and or someone disrespected me, I would use my words to express how I truly felt. Say one wrong word to me, disrespect me, my children and even my ex-husband and flames would spew. Not a proud moment, but since my assignment here is to bring transparency, accountability and encouragement to someone else, I won't go on and give the impression that the words that have rolled off my tongue were always filled with the Holy Spirit.

Verbal abuse was a part of my last relationship. All behind closed doors privately, often not feeling real. If I wasn't cursed at or called names, then someone must have been sick and did not have the energy to do the norm. Gut-wrenching, heart-aching, and as said in scripture, words that would pierce like swords. At first, I would stand and listen, but I always thought to myself, this is the first time I have ever had someone speak to me as often as they did in this manner. But as I thought that, did I do anything to change it? No. I had learned to overlook the unkindness, disrespect, indifference and disregard, and as a result, I did not stand up to him. I was constantly accused of cheating or our children not being his— which was ridiculous to hear because my routine was school, work, home for many years. I was on a strict curfew, isolated from everyone. And if the other wasn't busy committing adultery on their end, I was always in their sight. "I will be home in ten minutes." A minute later and my phone would repeatedly be ringing on end.

I was torn down verbally and degraded as a woman, wife, mother, sister and daughter. Honestly, as a human being as a whole. It truly didn't make sense how someone could speak to another in the manner they did daily. On the top of their lungs, in one's face and with zero apologies for their behaviour.

This needed to end. Staying in that relationship caused a lot of lasting effects on my physical and mental health and contributed immensely to my depression and anxiety. I was plagued with low self-esteem, mood swings, misplaced guilt, loneliness and isolation, to name a few. Despite being a natural night owl, I had trouble sleeping. I was filled with hopelessness, sadness, emptiness and I did not yearn for the relationship to get better. But the biggest regret I have for staying as long as I did, is how it was noticeably affecting our children. I no longer wanted to have to beg someone to lower their voice so their children did not have to hear the words spewing from deep down in their belly and out their mouth. Mind you, the response was always a firm and loud, "NO!" followed by, "Then don't be a (female dog)!" or "Your kids need to know who their mother is!" or "Then act like a woman!" etc. As much as I adored the tight squeezes from my children, I no longer wanted to have to console my kids for hours on end because of the chaos. I no longer wanted my eldest daughter to keep saying, "Mommy, just do what he wants," thinking this was normal in a marriage. I do take full responsibility for adding fuel to the fire by not biting my tongue at times when he spoke, but I did that for longer than I needed or should have.

My problems needed to be turned into solutions. I remember being severely broken in the middle of my living room, and I wailed out to our three in one God— The Father, the Son and the Holy Spirit.

"HELP ME"

I never knew my voice was as powerful as it was in that moment.

Every bit of my life when I felt it was falling apart, I laid it all out. I asked Him to comfort me and grant me compassion for and from my family. I found myself having daily conversations with God, asking him to show me how to understand and love myself the way he did.

Because I experienced an immense amount of verbal abuse, I wanted to ensure that the words I sent out to others, including my ex, would be words that healed others and not wounded them. **(Proverbs 12:18)** I no longer wanted to lose sight of myself and who God created me to be. I needed to ensure that I relied on God's strength to aid me regarding taming my tongue. I would ask for his forgiveness for any unloving words or attitudes I may have portrayed with or without knowing. I needed to ask the Holy Spirit to guide my heart, mind, speech and communication, honour Him in all my ways and help me speak words that will bring Him glory.

God gave us words to use for a good purpose. I want to encourage you, my friend, to steward your speech well and extend grace. It may seem impossible when you are at the other end of hateful speech from another. Still, no clearer verse reminds us of God's purpose of our words than a command from Paul to the Ephesians:

> *"Let no corrupt word proceed out of your mouth, but what is good for necessary edification, that it may impart grace to the hearers." - Ephesians 4:29 NKJV*

I acknowledge the damage the verbal abuse has caused me or another and admit to myself the position I was in. Respect, kind words, caring, empathy, understanding, warmth, appreciation and dignity was and still is all mine to have.

> *"Let your speech always be with grace, seasoned with salt, that you may know how you ought to answer each one." - Colossians 4:6 NKJV*

CHAPTER THIRTEEN

Purpose Recalculated

"Won't He Do It" - Koryn Hawthorne

I remember during a three hour drive home with my kids from a wonderful cottage getaway, behind the steering wheel, I had an overpowering urge to praise! So, I turned on my "Upbeat Worship Tunes" from my Spotify playlist, bopped my head and began to sing my heart out.

As we drove past open fields, the scenery was breathtaking to my left and my right. One look in front of us, no cars. One look into my rear-view mirror, not a car in sight. It was just a car filled with sleeping children, me and my God.

My playlist was hitting all the right places, and I would like to think that I was hitting all the right notes, but perhaps that is for another story to write.

But as I was driving, I was thinking about this book.

It was at that moment that I thought to myself, "Kerry-Ann, look at what God has brought you through, what He has brought you to and what He is about to do!" The tears were flowing, and I said, "My God! You are so faithful!"

The tears began to stream down my face. I always used to say, the life I had lived between the age of eighteen and the beginning of thirty-four, were only things you would see in a movie—a novel. And here you are, reading the book that I never imagined I would have the courage to write.

BUT GOD

An all-time favourite gospel artists' song began to play.

In Kirk Franklin's song "Love Theory," he sings how his most important achievement on the top of his list is to make God proud of him.

This book is just one of my faithful commitments to God. At the beginning of the book, I spoke about the importance of standing in obedience to God. I dodged and fought long enough, but my obedience to him surpasses all understanding. He reminded me that

> *"...he will restore everything you lost, he'll have compassion on you; he'll come back and pick up the pieces from all the places where you were scattered..."*
> **- Deuteronomy 30:3**

And my lifelong plan is to make him proud of me. If he were here with me face to face, I know the hugs, high fives, fist bumps, and victory dances between the two of us would be out of this world.

I never knew I would meet someone and be swept off my feet (or so I thought) at the tender age of seventeen.

I never knew that I would be an eighteen-year-old pregnant teen.

I never knew I would be a first-time mom shortly after my nineteenth birthday.

I never knew I would be a wife at the age of twenty-five.

I never knew I would be the owner of a successful licensed preschool.

I never knew I would be a mother again at the age of twenty-eight.

I never knew I would encounter depression and anxiety and be belittled for my condition.

I never knew that I would be a mom three times by the age of thirty-two.

I never knew there would be a dramatic shift in my spirituality and that one day, despite the slightly declined sense of hearing, that I would hear, with clarity and peace, God's instructions and plans.

I never knew that standing firm and obeying God's words would have me in the position that I am in today. And that includes all the many miraculous events, opportunities and favour I am and will continue to step into.

I never knew that I could be **free**.

CHAPTER FOURTEEN

The Best, Nothing Less

"He's Able" - Darwin Hobbs

What a mighty God we serve—with limitless power and overwhelming love.

My prayer is that this book has given someone hope. If you trust God with all your entirety, you will be a walking testimony of his goodness, just as I am. It's never too late to surrender your life to Him from head to toe. All that He has in store for you is closer than you think.

Relinquish control and give it all to Him, and trust Him in all your ways.

Your whole self, edified, is equipped with the armour of God, stand tall, know and believe that he is a man of his word! His promises are true and his mercies are new every day.

When you find yourself thinking of things that appear to be falling apart in your life, rest in God's words. Find peace knowing that they are actually falling in place, and some of your most complex trials will lead you to many amazing moments in your life. And he isn't done with you yet.

Be thankful, grateful and prepared to receive more than you have ever visioned and prayed for.

God gave me a good shake and the ability to forgive, heal, not settle, find, value and LOVE myself more than I ever have before. To bring me to newer and higher levels and most importantly, to get back right with Him than I have ever, ever been.

The one thing that has brought me through and will continue to is his grace and mercy. Although all these years have done wonders for me, I am thankful to the almighty for NEVER leaving my side and allowing me to say that although the past years were unfortunate, unsettling and traumatizing, I will POSITIVELY remember them. But the seconds, minutes, hours, days, months and years ahead will be undoubtedly better than the ones I have stepped out of.

I am claiming it all, fully covered in God's armour. I am a true walking testimony of what God has, can and will continue to do.

I encourage you to stay rooted and grounded in his promises. He is patient, kind and tender-hearted. He extends love time and time again when our heart is in pain and our stormy seasons come. Tell me, where would we be without God's great mercy? We all face different trials, so I encourage you to extend the mercy we have been shown, to those around you.

I am ever so thankful that God has given me the power to remain calm, peaceful and bloom where I am planted. I know that he is pushing me to go higher. He is taking me to different and higher levels in my life that I have not experienced before. Where he leads me, I will follow.

I moved from fear to joy with his guidance and have turned my mess into a message. I am here to tell you that you are no different. Time doesn't heal. God heals in his time and *always* on time. Despite our past and the challenges that lay ahead, we can ALWAYS beat the odds with God as our strength.

Do not doubt.

Do not waver.

Do not fear.

Just have faith.

Self-care is important for our growth. Allow God to shift your perspective and allow yourself from time to time to treat yourself to some of the simple things that you love in life—guilt free.

Be thankful and always give God the glory.

At times, you will feel as if you are out in the deep. But the steps you used to take—treading lightly, walking softly, tip-toeing in and around things and people, not wanting to ever step on anyone's toes—will come to pass once you commit and surrender your darkness to God from head to toe. More than often, it is when circumstances appear the most impossible, that is where God's glory shines the brightest. When you make that decision and put your foot down, quite literally, your walk will become an entire liberating vibe on its own.

I encourage you to **_Proverbs 3:5_** and to walk in God's will with courage and fire under your feet.

God only has the absolute best for us and nothing less.

CHAPTER FIFTEEN

Abundant Life, Access Granted, More In Store

"Promises" - Maverick City

Forever in a posture of gratitude to the one who was, is, and will be with me throughout my most challenging trials.

In my devastation, His name was the only name I could utter.

He has heard my cries and always answers with this sweet refrain.

Always healing and giving me indescribable peace and joy.

Taking <u>everything</u> to God in prayer.

And still, I long to trust him more.

CHAPTER SIXTEEN

No Distance In Prayer

"Goodness Of God" - CeCe Winans

I pray that this book and your days ahead will grant you with the desires of your heart. And if it doesn't, have crazy faith that it will. Our desires are only crazy until it happens. The power of prayer is real. You just need faith as small as a mustard seed **(Matthew 17:20)** to see his marvelous works. I pray that you may find the strength to leave behind negative mindsets and make room for the unimaginable increases in your life.

Seasons will change, but our God still reigns. It won't always be easy, but it will always be worth the wait. I pray that his shield will cover you. I pray that you will gain courage, revelations, confirmations, signs and wonders. I declare that God is enlarging your territory, in the name of the Father, the Son and the Holy Spirit, amen.

We will encounter unimaginable torrential storms, experience anger when things don't work out the way we planned or when expectations in life seem to fail us. But rather than drift, stay anchored and trust our Creator. He orchestrates things in our lives for the good. He will move people or things out of your path so you can, with your entirety, rely on him in times of trouble.

Trust the process and trust that God will show up in ways you would never expect. Glow. That glow hits different when God turns that pain into peace. Always stand with your armour of God on. Portray the fruits of the spirit. If convicted, repent. The Holy Spirit will always convict us if we fall short of his glory. Seek God in all your ways. He saves. He heals. He provides. He promises. He never leaves his own.

YOU ARE DESERVING, WORTHY, LOVED

And because of Him, His grace and His mercy, just like I strive to be… You are oh so **F.A.B.**

Many blessings to you. Peace, healing, perfect health, continued love or finding thereof. Excellent health, miracles, breakthroughs, provision, favour exceedingly and abundantly than you have ever imagined.

I'm sending you lots of love, hugs, and prayers from the bottom of my heart.

SURVIVOR, WARRIOR,

Faithful, Anchored, Blessed

Kerry-Ann

PEACE - BROKEN CHAINS - FREEDOM - VICTORY

"Brighter Day" - Kirk Franklin

... I JUST WANT TO THANK YOU LORD!

ABOUT THE AUTHOR

Kerry-Ann Facey lives in Toronto, Ontario.

She is the proud mother of three beautiful children: Kasia, Kalista and Kyzic.

She has been an entrepreneur since 2011.

Her obedience to God and doing work for the kingdom is her passion. Kerry-Ann hopes to use her experiences and voice as a platform to bless others. She hopes that through her humbleness and transparency of sharing a small dose of her story, she will sow and extend encouragement to others to walk boldly in their faith. With the wisdom she has gained throughout her struggles and will continue to gain throughout her rewarding walk with Christ, Kerry-Ann strives to be... **F.A.B. (Faithful. Anchored. Blessed)**

@faithfulanchoredblessed
faithfulanchoredblessed@gmail.com

www.ingramcontent.com/pod-product-compliance
Lightning Source LLC
Chambersburg PA
CBHW020914080526
44589CB00011B/598